PATHWAYS OF LIFE

PATHWAYS OF LIFE

Deloris Goins

with the assistance of

Dorothy Rockett

Lulu Press 2006

Copyright © 2006 Deloris Williams Goins
and Dorothy Zwier Rockett

Post-manuscript design, layout, and
production by Andrew M. Rockett.

Typeset using the LaTeX 2_ε typesetting
system created by Leslie Lamport
and Peter Wilson's *memoir* class.

Cover art by Norman E. Goins, Jr.

10 9 8 7 6 5 4 3 2   Corrected 20060828

Acknowledgments

We are grateful for the artistic recipe illustrations drawn by Brenda Jackson Desobry, the niece of the dentist mentioned in this story. She formerly taught art in the Charlottesville school system. She now resides in Texas with her family.

DR is Dorothy Rockett who recorded and edited Deloris' words. With the expertise and enthusiasm of Anne Sloop, the words of these remembrances entered the computer world of floppies. We can never thank her enough. Our hats are also off to Judy Bazin who transferred large type printing into upper and lower case computer reality.

Deloris Williams Goins

Foreword

Deloris came into my life just as my vision began to vanish. She drives my car—so that's one thing my guardian angel need not be concerned about any more. We do errands and shop together. Between her checking labels and prices, we talk, sharing trivia, ideas and dreams.

"I want to write a book," she tells me. "I have lots of stories to tell."

And so she does, from tales of cracking black walnuts at the kitchen table in her Grandfather's farm house to having her picture published in a well-known photographer's books.

"I'll tell you one day why I'm scared of cats," she says, eyeing my white angora puss who wants to be friends.

Now that day is here and the stories begin.

DR

Dorothy Zwier Rockett

Contents

Acknowledgments   v

Foreword   vii

1   Grandpa's Farm   1

2   Farm Acres   7

3   Early Learning   9

4   Gospel Songs   15

5   Downtown Doings   19

6   Where Did We Shop?   23

7   Back to the Classroom   27

8   Studying Again   33

9   Other School Essays   37

10   Leaving School Behind   45

CONTENTS

11	Finding Family	49
12	Children and More Children	53
13	When We Were Young	55
14	New Crossroads	59
15	Dreams	65
16	Recipes, Past and Present	67
	Spoon Bread	67
	Fried Green Tomatoes	68
	Fried Fresh Corn	69
	Fish-for-Dinner	70
	Hoe Cakes	71
	Wild Game	72
	Scrambled Eggs and Pork Brains	73
	Fried Potatoes with Scrambled Eggs	73
	Chicken Feet Stew	74
	Corn Bread	74
	Pie Crust	75
	Sweet Potato Pie	75
	Pound Cake	76
	Doris's Cream Puffs	77

Afterward   79

1

Grandpa's Farm

MY Grandpa's farm was a wondrous place. The two tulip poplar trees in front of the house just about reached the sky. They were the only things taller than Grandpa, it seemed to me. He called me Sister Lulu or Baby Sis, but my name really is Deloris. There was a cold spring of clear waters, some chickens, pigs and a cow, big stacks of wood for Grandma's stove, which never had the fire go out, and a creek to stick bare feet in on a hot summer day.

This is where my sister Doris and I lived for the first several years of our lives, because Mama and Daddy were super busy working all the time in Charlottesville. They came to the farm on weekends, bringing grocery staples like sugar and flour for Grandma to use in cooking meals for all of us. Later our younger sisters Devone and Diane were also at the farm before going to school.

The farm was in Eastham, Virginia north of Charlottesville. There was enough land for kinfolks to build a house down the hollow, another around the bend in the lane, and still leave eight acres for planting vegetables. He grew squash, snap and pole beans, potatoes, cucumbers, green peas, tomatoes, turnips, lots of greens. Grandpa, Uncle Willie and Uncle Jim used hand plows to break the earth. The two plows had wooden handles attached to pointed iron wedges. Other tools were just hoes. I helped put three corn kernels in each line when Grandpa plowed. Grandpa earned money picking apples and peaches in the orchards near home. There was no running water in the house, no screens on the windows and no electricity. There was a two seater outhouse way in the back.

There was also a shed where Grandma had a big trunk. One day she went there and when she opened the trunk a huge black snake wrapped itself around her. She fell back in a dead faint after hollering. Uncle Willie and Uncle Jim found her and went on a snake hunt to kill him. They shot him and hung his monster body, thick as a man's arm, in a tree.

"How did you watch TV?'" my own grandkids ask today. "No video games?" They don't believe me when I tell them I was too busy "doing things" to have time to play very much. I did make mud pies under the tulip trees using Grandma's Mason jar lids for baking tins.

Grandpa gave me my very own tool: a hammer-hatchet tool. Grandpa always kept my hatchet real sharp. He had a grinding wheel with a pedal so he could turn it fast, the knives steady on the stone. When the pedal broke, he made a handle to turn it. He was very skilled at holding a knife or my hatchet in one hand and turning the stone with the other. I don't know why, but the hatchet always cut the kindling, never my fingers or toes.

Uncle Willie and my nephew Toby at the farm using Grandpa's grinding stone.

I used the hammer side when we cracked black walnuts and the hatchet side when I made kindling for Grandma's stove. It was a big, black monster with an oven and warming shelves, and places for pots to boil and chicken to fry. Grandpa always said grace before our meals, ending with a big "a-a-a-men, let's eat."

Grandma was as tiny as Grandpa was tall, a person of boundless energy. She worked canning, cleaning, and always cooking. She took in washing and ironing. Her flatiron was heated on the stove. For washing she used yellow Octagon soap and rubbed clothes against a corrugated wash board. Water was stored in two big cisterns. Most of the time they had mosquitoes floating on top—we called them wiggle-tails.

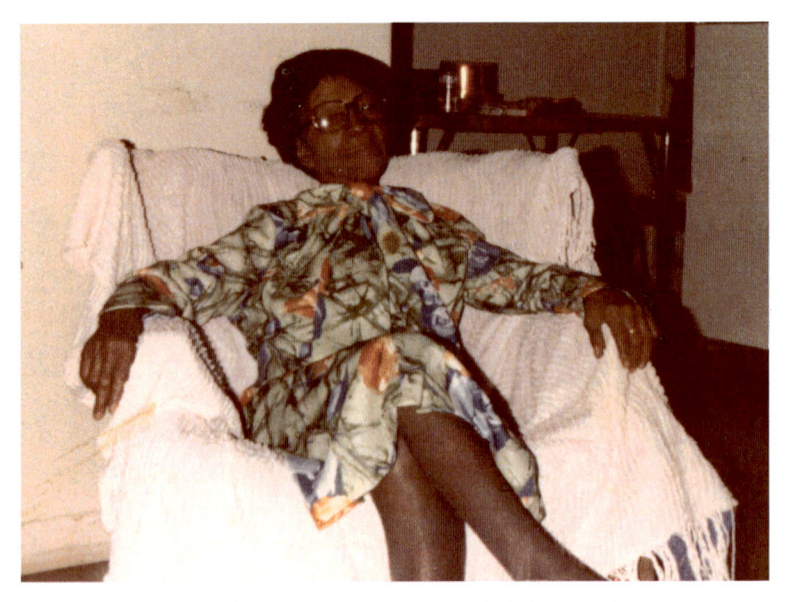

Grandma in later years in her home at 726 Prospect Avenue.

Once Grandma was very naughty—or determined. She washed and ironed a white blouse noting that it was "just her size." "Well," she said, "I just wanted to look real pretty going to church" (which was Chapman Grove Baptist). So she wore it just once, came home and washed and ironed it with a secret smile on her face.

This was the 1950s, not the 1850s, and there was but one contact with the outside world: a radio, powered by a huge battery. Everyone gathered to listen and laugh with "Amos and Andy."

Another job I had was collecting eggs. There was a chicken coop but mostly the hens ranged free. I watched one particular bird going under the house again and again. So one day I followed, crawling in a small space under the house. Sure enough there was a nest. I was proud to find it, but when I tried to back out, I got stuck. I cried and screamed, kicked and screamed. Of course it was my Grandpa who found me. "Sister Lulu," he said as he cut off the top of my braid which was snagged on a nail. "Don't you ever do that again!" I didn't.

Then I went to play with my mud pies and Grandpa sat on the porch steps, lighting his corn cob pipe. He always had a red can of Prince Albert Tobacco and a can of Duke's Mixture tobacco. Sometimes Duke's came in a small gunny sack, about six inches high. It was tied on the end. Grandma used these sacks to keep her money safe.

Did I tell you we had 20 or so pigs? They gobbled up table scraps and Grandpa used to hitch a ride to Love's Grove Mill on Garrett Street in Charlottesville to buy pig feed. When the cold weather came, it was time to get food for the winter. So lots of kin came and either by shot or knife the killing was done. Water boiled in great kettles. A table was set up for the quartering. Hams were salted and hung by nail in the smokehouse. We children went a million times to the spring for fresh water because it was up to us to clean out the intestines—squeaky clean. Sounds awful? Sure, but the chittlins sure tasted good later on.

Grandma's name was Viola Rosa Taylor and she came from Simeon. Grandpa was Stewart Charles Smith of Eastham. Their children were Charles Jr., Dorothy (my Mama) and William (my Uncle Willie). Her mother was Kitty Waites and her father was Horace Taylor. He was a preacher. Viola and her sisters Sadie, Agnes, Hallie, and Louise sang gospel hymns. The girls used to laugh and joke: "We ain't no hand-me downs. We Taylor made girls!"

2

Farm Acres

GRANDPA'S farm came to him from his parents, Annie Lee Smith and Ferrell Smith. The many acres were on both sides of Route 769, Rocky Hollow Road. I had lots of kinfolk because Grandpa had five sisters: Roberta, Lilly, Annie, Rachel, and Susie. His six brothers were: Ferrell, Jr., Johnny, Marshal, Benjamin, Samson, and Isaiah.

Even though the family was so big, Grandma always joined Grandpa in telling them all that they could build houses on the acres, but they couldn't sell the land. "Ours is ours" she always said. It stays in the family. "Ours is ours" is still a refrain in my mind.

I remember looking over "ours" after I'd climbed a hilltop (mountain to me) where I came to some flat rocks—my favorite place to see everything under the blue sky. "Where have you been so long?" Grandma would ask me. I just said "out" and "I'm back now."

I still try to visit one special part of the property, a

quiet place up on the hill where the family cemetery is. Although it is over-grown with greens, the stone markers are there, recording the names and dates of the Smiths and their kin.

3

Early Learning

AT the end of one summer, I remember Mama told me to leave my country clothes at the farm because I would be wearing city clothes for the next few months. It was the worst day of my life. I was going to have to go to school.

My first grade teacher was Mrs. Ophelia Smith at Jefferson, a segregated school. I cried buckets all that first day—and so did the other girl next to me.

We went by bus and stayed all day, 8:30 until 3:00. We ate lunch there and the food was good because there were good cooks in the kitchen, but it never tasted like Grandma's—her hoecakes and peach preserves or blackberry jam. And Grandpa wasn't asking me, "What do you want for breakfast Baby Sis?" I'd say, "Chicken and fried corn!" "Well, go pick an ear," he'd tell me and I'd run outside to pick an ear of corn for him to shuck. Grandma would heat ham grease in the skillet, cut down the corn kernels, and fry them crisp. Oh, it tasted so good!

But school got a lot better and I made friends. We learned the usual basics and had Virginia history, gym and science. For that, we planted and watched seedlings grow. I knew more than anybody about that, because I had helped Grandpa plant vegetables.

Art? Yes. We had Mrs. McClum for drawing, finger painting, paper-mache stuff. And for music, Calvin Cage taught us to sing songs. He had a red music box to play some songs for us. There was no piano in our classroom. He also conducted the band at Jefferson.

When I got to seventh grade, I had a real important job: I was a safety patrol girl with a badge to wear and an orange vest.

I'm full of "I remembers." Two events during third grade stay with me always. One was a party Mrs. Smith gave for us. Her husband came to school carrying two big jars, one under each arm. They were filled with something wonderful, something I'd never tasted before: tuna fish and macaroni salad! I ate and ate.

The other important happening was a PTA meeting. Mr. Booker T. Reeves, the principal, was in charge and there was someone to play the piano when I sang. I can still sing the words:

> A long time back in history some boys began to tease,
> That's why it is a mystery that spread like some disease.
> At first he teased Sister Smart and often made her cry,
> Will someone tell me why, oh why?
> Why I wonder why are boys forever teasing?
> Why are girls forever teased?
> Why do boys get so much pleasure just to make girls

displeased?
Someday it will all be different and things will be just the reversed,
When girls decide to do the teasing, boys will get it all the worse.

There was a lot of applause when I made my bow.

While I was great at softball and shooting marbles, I hated gym class because I couldn't tumble or climb ropes. Two things about gym were good though. I had my own set of clothes. The white pants came to the knees and had a blue stripe down the sides. Cool! Cool also was our teacher, Edward Hawkins. He was real handsome!

Mama and Daddy's house at 519 Sixth Street SE.

We lived at 519 Sixth Street SE. My daddy, Hubert Allen Williams, known as Buster, worked full time in the machine shop at Frank Ix Company, and on weekends he was the night watchman. I went around the building once while he tested locks and it was very dark and very scary. My Mama, Dorothy May, worked in laundries, Clark School cafeteria, and watched over neighbors' kids at home. She also started a bakery making sweet potato pies and cakes for people. In addition to me and Doris, there were Diane and Devone to take care of. Brother Archie was by this time a grown man, done military service, and was living next door with his wife and two sons. We went with her every month to pay the mortgage on our house. Later when we knew the way, she would give one of us an envelope containing $40, instructing us to go to the top floor of the National Bank and Trust building (now Wachovia). "Run all the way and don't drop the money," she'd say.

There are more Jefferson School "I remembers." Each week we would take our dime or our dimes to school because it was time to buy stamps, saving for a U.S. Bond. When the stamp book was filled we took it to the post office, now Jefferson Madison Regional Library. We went in the back entrance of the building. I always felt sorry for some kids who didn't have a dime at any time all the year.

At school I recall Mr. Smart, our custodian, who made us all look smart about keeping his school as neat as neat could be. He really had standards and some of the kids didn't like him. I did. Mr. Smart lived near Jefferson School on Brown Street. On this street was a city jail, called Brown's Jail. The building stood where city yard now is located. I remember seeing inmates at the windows, hollering down to us. We always waved back and sometimes if we knew each other, we carried messages home for them.

Back at Jefferson School there was Mrs. Woodfolk in the kitchen. Sometimes we had Breyers ice cream in little cups where we found a vanilla bean. I never went to the public library, just used the books in school.

One great holiday program was on May Day when I wore my best dress even though we had relay races for fun. When springtime came that first school year, I could hardly wait for the term to end. Then my sister Doris and I could go back to the farm where the red rambler roses blanketed the entrance road. Lilacs bloomed beside the porch and honeysuckle vines covered everything. The blossoms were so good to suck. Sometimes we would climb into the willow tree branches to hide in a feathery green world. There were apple, peach and cherry trees thick with blossoms.

I also thought about Grandpa's sister, Aunt Roberta. Now she lived in a grand house on Park Street with very rich people. On most Thursday afternoons we could hardly wait for her, watching for Pace's Taxi to come up the farm lane. She always had lots of big brown bags with her. We'd yell, "smothering pans, smothering pans" when we ran to meet her. She'd sit like a queen at the kitchen table watching us enjoy the food she had brought. We would never have tasted roast beef except for her. After three hours, the taxi would return and back she went to the grand house and her lifetime job. She never married and she never forgot us.

Mama playing her miniature piano.

4

Gospel Songs

IN our house there was always gospel music. Mama had a portable piano on which she played hymns. She was a Pentecostal Church of God preacher, and she spread the gospel words all the time. In fact, some folks called her "jukebox" because she never stopped. One time she had a revelation. Doris and I stood at the top of the stairs and saw her stretched out on the floor yelling "Don't you see it? Don't you see the light? A big yellow ball it is, and the doorway is all lit up." We didn't see it but we did see her face all bluish and strange.

Sometimes when she preached on the streets she would take us with her. We never slept in on Saturdays. At 6:30 a.m. sharp, she would pound out gospel songs and it was time to start the day. We had to clean our rooms neat and tidy before she gave us a dime each and we were free to spend it at the store and go out to play.

Mama, who was married when she was 16, said she was looking for guidance and peace in her life. So she went to a tent revival meeting in Charlottesville. The preachers were the Reverend Marvin Gaye, father of the singer Marvin Gaye, and Bishop Rawlings. Later she took us children to the Reverend C. H. Brown's Church of God in Christ on Rosser Avenue. We all piled

into J. T. Graves yellow cab which took us there for 25 cents, a special price for church on Sundays. There was a 10 a.m. Sunday school, church service at noon, and after a short snack break another service in the afternoon. Mama's strong contralto voice and piano playing would "light the church up!" There were guitars, drums, tambourines, and wash boards to give rhythm to the shouting and dancing and speaking in unknown tongues. Mama could sway a congregation with her singing, especially when she sang "What is This." Everybody would be on their feet, praising God when she sang. The spirit filled the church.

I can sing the words, even now. And I can hear Kenneth Coles sing it, too. I have his CD, "I'm Ready". The CD cover mentions thanks to: "Archie Williams for the original recording of 'What is This' and to your mom, Dorothy Williams, for the inspiration. No one can sing 'What is This' the way you can."

Here are the words which touched so many people.

What is This

> What is this,
> I can feel deep down inside,
> What is this,
> That keeps setting my soul on fire,
> Whatever it is, it won't let me hold my peace.
> What is this,
> That make folk say I'm acting strange,
> What is this,
> That make me love to call God's name,
> Whatever it is, it won't let me hold my peace.
> I know it makes me love my enemies,
> Oh! It makes me love my friends,
> And it won't let me be ashamed
> To tell the world that I've been born again.
> Oh! What is this,
> That's got me feeling so good right now,
> What is this,
> That makes me want to run on anyhow,
> Whatever it is, Oh! It won't let me hold my peace.

Little did I know that just as my sisters and I sang in a performing group, my own children would be members of a choir singing gospel music. It was much, much later, 1992 in fact, when the Charlottesville Community Youth Choir was started by Teresa Michie

Jones and her friend, Marcia Jones. The first concert was in December 1992, followed by many more at churches in the area. They sang in the Mount Zion Baptist Church as part of the First Night Virginia program. My kids were part of the 40 member choir. How sweet their voices were. And they so enjoyed the organ, keyboard accompaniment. One of their favorite songs was "It Will Be All Right." They rocked it.

Mama and my sister Doris often sang at church.

Mama founded the Joy Gospel Singers who performed not only in Charlottesville but in Gordonsville, Standardsville, and Quinque. The members included Carol Lee Jones, Thelma Grady, Doris Minor, myself and my sisters, Diane and Devone. Ernestine Slaughter was the pianist. Mama never studied religion but she would read Bible verses and just begin to speak. She did not know where all the words came from—except from God. Later in her life she conducted services in the front parlor of her home in Fifeville.

5

Downtown Doings

IN grade school and later at Burley High, we all liked the movies on Main Street (now the Mall). There were the Lafayette, Jefferson and Paramount Theatres. At the first two, we could go in the front entrance, but immediately had to climb the wooden stairs to the balcony, where the seats were almost falling apart and the springs sticking out. At the Paramount there was a side entrance for us, a door painted green. Collecting ticket money was Mrs. Elmer Sampson, wife of the Burley music teacher, and also Punny Wigginton. He kept order in the balcony. I remember sometimes going there in the summer for 25 cent matinees, just for kids. We could sit downstairs after a period of time, but often went back to our familiar spot, the balcony.

There was another place with a back door for us. When we hitched a ride to town with Grandma and Grandpa, we stopped for a hotdog at the C & O restaurant. It was a railroad eatery and we sat on empty soda crates at a rickety table in a small storage room. "Cowboy" served us the dogs and french fries. We called him cowboy because he wore a big hat, boots, and chaps! This was the time when cars parked on Main Street and Tippy Rhodes tap danced up and down the sidewalks. He was lots of fun and always wanted to make people smile. I knew him because he lived at 407 Sixth Street SE next to my grandfather. His mother was Miss Maggie and his sister, Jiggy, and his brother, Big Man. He used to shoo us back home when he saw us near the railroad tracks.

Clarence Tippy Rhodes was mentioned in a 1979 article "Folklore and Folk Life in Virginia". Helen Davis described his dancing: "He'd dance over to the gutter and hop up and down off the sidewalk, or kind of scoot around in a circle. He never used his hands or anything but his feet. Sometimes he would pretend his feet were running away from under him. And he would say funny things about the people watching him, so they would start to throw money. He'd run around after it while he was still dancing." I have a Daily Progress story in the July 21, 1997 issue which tells about the finding and burial of his ashes. He passed in 1992.

Our favorite playground was "the bottom," a grassy hollow between Sixth and Fifth Streets SE. That's where Garrett Square is now. Mama lost her house to the city planners. It was a nice house with paneled walls and with a green and white striped awning outside—the only one on the block. My family moved to Grove Street in Fifeville, but that was after I left Burley.

Another playground, Flint's Field, was where we played softball, kickball, football, and where our parents and grandparents came to watch our games on Sunday afternoons. We shot marbles there, sometimes all day long. "Tarp" was what we called the biggest shooter marble. I could propel it so fast it would split a small marble in two! There were surrounding trees and shrubs for hide-and-seek games, and where we cut long sticks to make stick horses. We cut designs in them and had a hitching post to park our horses when their run was over. I carved mine with pinto spots. There was a grove of Osage orange trees there. The big green wrinkled fruits we called milk balls and boy what a milk ball fight we would have with other kids from over Ware Street!

22　PATHWAYS OF LIFE

Deloris and Doris, taken across from Marguerite's and near the Stucco House.

6

Where Did We Shop?

WELL, there was Allen's store near where we lived (he had good pork chops, cut thin like Mama ordered), Estes on Cherry Avenue, and Stop and Shop on Main Street. When we came to town with Grandma she bought things there too. There were always folks to greet on Main Street and often when Grandma was talking, people would notice me, saying "what a pretty little girl." They'd give me quarters and dimes and often as not we would have the fare to take a taxi back to the farm. Going home from Jefferson School, we'd get ginger snaps for a penny apiece at Mr. Inge's grocery. Rock-and-roll cakes had pink icing and were five cents.

We'd walk past the Bible Way Church on Vinegar Hill where the Reverend Frank Jackson was the preaching man. But we'd hurry fast past the taverns.

Mama took us to the Victory Shoe Store, owned and tended by Tilly Miller. She'd tell Mama "it's okay" when she heard there was only a dollar to spend. She'd write it on a card and we'd pay her next time. She never sent a bill or refused us a pair of shoes. Once Mama baked her a birthday cake and we all sang "Happy Birthday, Miss Tilly." She was so surprised!

Miss Fay, Miss Tilly and Mama at the Victory Shoe Store birthday party.

At the back of her store, she had a bargain table where Mama once chose a pair of green sandals for me. I hated them and cried and howled about it all the way home, on and off for several days. When Sunday came and I just had to wear those awful things, I found that the heels had been sawed off! Mama blamed me, but I didn't do it and my sister Doris didn't either. My Daddy just walked out of the house, and we never did know who did it. Mama picked out another bargain pair but they were really no improvement. And I was unhappy about them for a long time.

Just about the time I graduated from Jefferson, electricity came to Grandpa's farm. There was a light now in every room, but the big black stove was still the heart of the kitchen. And the Kent stoves still heated each of the bedrooms with wood fires. My Mama bought lots of things for the house over the years. Most important was a pink and white Sears and Roebuck washing machine. It stood on the side porch ready to help Grandma. The only trouble was that, having no money to dig a well, all the water for the machine had to be carried up from the stream or hauled out of the cisterns to make it run, but run it did!

Grandma sitting in her kitchen at the farm house.

Electricity brought great happenings to the farm. If you had "juice" you could plug in your electric guitars. Uncle Willie, George Minor and Allen Blakey did. Mama's portable piano was on hand, played by Dog Kenney, with Big Jimbo on drums. The singer was Lewis Toliver. The air was pounded with rock and roll, blues, and soul rhythms on weekends. You could hear them over on Stony Point Road! Everybody came and Grandma was sure busy frying chicken. They were real good times. I can still tap my feet when I remember songs like "Honey Dripper," "Walkin' the Dog," "Raunchy," "Hideaway," and "I Got a Woman Way 'Cross Town."

7

Back to the Classroom

THIS time I attended Burley High School, another segregated center. It drew students from Albemarle County, Buckingham and Greene. I had friends finally from all over the area, especially Scottsville, Crozet and Ivy. Riding the bus for an hour or more in the morning and again to return home was part of every school day. I hated chemistry with those awful Bunsen burners, but loved art and music. Waldo Johnson, our art teacher, taught us pastels, watercolor, charcoal, pencil sketching and ceramics. We had exhibits in the hall every year and Mr. Johnson had some oil paintings displayed permanently in the building. I sang in the choir and my sister Doris played the clarinet in the band, conducted by Elmer Sampson. They were famous!

We didn't pay any attention to Lane High School and its white students! It didn't interest us. Our football team played schools as far away as Halifax. We had fun at Carver Recreation Center at the back of Jefferson School where we roller skated and there were arts and crafts. Dorothy Palmer, Margaret Stroud, and Mrs. Waldo Johnson ran the center. Best of all were our dances, some formal and some sock hops. We had our very own dance bands. Musicians included Junny Gohaner, David Dickerson, and Tony Martin. They played rock and roll and soul music on drums, saxophones, electric guitars. The place was jumping!

Now as I recall pastimes, I realize how segregated, how separated we really were. I don't think I had any idea either of how many dedicated white people in Charlottesville were trying to solve problems in the Virginia Massive Resistance Period. I had no idea until recently that a cross had been burned on the property of Sarah Patton Boyle, author of "The Desegregated Heart." I did know about my own peoples' effort for justice. Mama knew black activists including ministers with whom she was acquainted: the Rev. Reginald Johnson, Drewery Brown, Eugene Williams, Raymond Bell, Jesse Williams, Rev. Henry Mitchell, Rev. Henry Floyd Johnson, and Rev. B.F. Bunn and his wife.

It was after high school that my friends and I would meet on Main Street—this time to eat at Woolworth's lunch counter. Sometimes we would be followed by white boys, speaking insults and slurs about us. We had to pretend not to hear, but just continue on—a little bit faster, faster on our way. Grandpa in the country always had good friends, black and white. It didn't matter. They had coffee at kitchen tables and talked and joked together. But somehow things cooled in small country communities too. "I just know honey," he would tell me, "When you roll back the skin, everybody looks the same underneath." Our Mama reminded us that when God created man he made a flower garden, filled with all different colors, different shapes and different sizes. "Weeds grow up amid the flowers," she would say. "Don't let the weeds choke your good flowers, look beyond that."

When I was 14 years old and a sophomore, a really, really great thing happened to me. Daddy took me to Judge Hamlett in the Midway Building to get a permission paper for me to take my driver's test. We went to Russell Mooney's car dealership and he bought a black 1954 Oldsmobile 98. It had "wings" at the back and I knew I was going to fly. I took my driving test at the DMV down the hill on High Street. There were two logs lined up on the lot where you had to park your car. Blanche Henderson, a friend, took me there in her big Buick. I can still hear her saying, "Watch the wings." So now we didn't depend on the bus and I drove my sister and my friends to school.

I was able to drive Mama around on errands and even go out to Eastham and take Grandpa and Grandma for little joy rides. Before school on weekdays I got up real early in order to take Aunt Sadie, Aunt Hallie and Mama to the City Laundry where they started work at 7:30 a.m.

Studying continued and I took two years of typing under Miss Gloria Thaxton who later taught my daughter typing. Only this time it was not at Burley, but at Charlottesville High School. Strict discipline was maintained both at Jefferson and Burley. No foolishness was tolerated. "You were a different person when you left the class." That also meant you left the threat of a ruler on your palm.

When I was in Burley, I went to have my hair "done" at a very special place. It was the Carver Inn, a hotel and restaurant for black people, the only such place in the city. A big white painted house with columns and a veranda, it sat high on Preston Avenue, just west of the railroad bridge and tracks. Mrs. Beatrice Fowlkes was the proprietor. Tables with pretty linens and working fireplaces welcomed the famous and not so famous to fish fry dinners. Louis Armstrong and Hattie McDaniel and many others stayed there. Carver Inn also had a cosmetology school. Women gathered in rooms at the back of the inn learning to cut and arrange hair, give facials and manicures. I can remember a record called "Fannie Mae" on the jukebox there. Buster Brown was the singer. It sounded good!

I suppose everyone falls in love sometime—maybe more than once. It happened to me when I was in my last year of high school. I wore my diamond ring to class. I was going to marry George William Minor, a Burley graduate who had completed military service, a hitch in the U.S. Marines. He was working now in the post office. Our wedding (against Mama's advice) was on May 14, 1966. I became a housewife, dropping out of school because of frustrations with one particular course and teacher. After several years, we separated and I had jobs at several places: Badger Powhatan, Chemetron on Ivy Road and General Electric.

The years just after my marriage were less than

restful. And it was not only for me, but for all of Charlottesville. There were racial slurs and tensions and "disturbances." I saw the Safeway Super Market on West Main Street on fire. Police and fire engines came, and groups of young black men from the Westhaven housing development were rocking and overturning cars. It was frightening to watch as I did one night on the corner of Ninth Street where a car with white people was rocked. I ran to Mama's—down to Grove Street and away from the sirens.

Also sometime during these years I went for my first visit to one of the "good times houses" in the black community. The tradition is still alive and kicking in Charlottesville. You went there for fun—to meet people, hear stereo music, buy hard liquor by the shot, the pint, or the bottle. They all were and even now are in private houses. Big money, really big money is part of the scene. Dice are rolled and bets placed. Cards are dealt for five card and seven card poker. And the fastest hottest game is Georgia skins. Sometimes you can bet and win thousands of dollars. Sometimes you can lose your car. But you keep coming back for more.

The dealer in Georgia skins is a fast talking man who whips up emotions as he shuffles the cards. Standing around the table six or eight men draw a card from the pack. They bet against the drawn cards, trusting "their kind of card" be it a two or a king or an ace will not be slid out of the deck. If a match happens, you are "out" and have to pay out all your fifty, hundred or two hundred dollar bets. I only watched but two of my sisters went to those houses many times.

You know black people may not have much, but they know how to have a great night of fun and laughter. On Fridays at Lonnie's there was a fish fry. At most places you could eat great fried chicken and potato salad. Cars started lining up Thursday nights, and then it was Friday, Saturday and Sunday too.

Down on Main Street, up above where the M.C. Thomas Furniture Store was located, there was a gambling den for many years. Of course the numbers racket thrived and still goes on today. Money was linked to operations in Washington, D.C. and Maryland. I know because once I bet on the number 333 and won over $250.

8

Studying Again

I did return to school and—you won't believe this—received my diploma from Albemarle High School. This was so much later, it was 1990. Everybody talked to each other and there were no hard feelings among the students and teachers. I could never have gone to a white school as a teenager. It was too hard to even think about, so perhaps it was just as well as things turned out. In 1990, I only had two courses to complete for my diploma: government, in which I received an A-, and English, which I aced. On compositions I submitted Mr. Julian Taylor wrote a note: "Your writing is excellent." I wrote from my heart. I wrote: "I wanted to tell about where I grew up. Some people called it 'the Road' or 'Chinatown' and said bad things about the people who lived there." So I wrote, "The one thing they didn't know is that people in that area stuck together. If one family had a problem, everybody had a problem until it could be resolved. We never had to hire babysitters because everybody took care of everybody's children. We had preachers who would come out on Saturdays and preach on the street corners. We had Miss Lou Williams, Big Maybelle, and Mary Alice when people wanted to party and have a good time. Miss Lou had socials every week and charged 25 cents to get in. I had such a wonderful time, I wished it still existed, but they tore down a lot of the houses to build Garrett Square. All of those 'uptown' people who used to talk about the road are living there now. They are the ones who gave my home a bad name. It's funny how things turn out."

Garrett Square has the same name as the most wonderful man, Dr. Marshall T. Garrett. He took care of all the black community for miles around. His office was on Main Street across from the Midway Building. You could see him there but most of the day and night he was out on house calls, prescribing medicine in a gentle way and encouraging with kind words. I remember when I was little, I passed out at the breakfast table. It was a seizure. Mama prayed for "the blood of Jesus" to save me. Dr. Garrett said I would be all right. Mama kept right on praying. Later on one day I was home from school because I didn't feel well. By and by I got up and went to the closet to get some clothes. It happened again. I woke up laying face down, my head on the closet floor. That was the last time the seizure hit me. Dr. Garrett and Mama were right.

Another kind gentleman took care of us. He was Dr. Elard Jackson whose dental office was at 125 Fourth Street SW. We used to go in the side entrance on Commerce Street where we sat in his chair. He looked big as a giant. With his big hand on your head, believe me you didn't move an inch and did exactly as he asked you to do.

I also wrote essays about Grandma's passing at Martha Jefferson Hospital. It was Easter day and I had been to Easter service. I had been trying to nap, but my baby was twisting and turning and keeping me awake. I knew why I was not sleeping. It was Grandma. So I urged Mama and my sister to come with me. We were in time to say the Lord's Prayer at her bedside. I often wondered if my baby knew what was happening. I couldn't stop thinking about Grandma and the sadness knowing her time to pass had come. My mind kept churning with remembrances of her and my own "time to come" in the University of Virginia Hospital. I had had surgery for a deviated septum and gone home to my apartment on Thirteenth Street NW only to have terrible headaches, dizziness and coldness. I got up and went across the railroad tracks to the hospital, down this little path by this big mountain of coal. Tons and tons of coal were piled up all the way and I thought I would pass out and no one would find me if the coal covered me up. I got to the emergency room and was told I'd have to have a spinal tap. Well, they did two, but sent me home because they could find nothing wrong. But about midnight, Mama and Dad came to take me back to the hospital, because doctors had called and told them I was sick and could die. I had an infection in my spinal cord. My temperature climbed to 103 degrees, went down, came up again over two weeks. I had faith in the doctors, but I knew that the Head Doctor could do the job for me and get me well—I am talking about Doctor Jesus. Early one morning about 4 o'clock I started praying to Jesus like I had never prayed before. I closed my eyes in that dark room and lay still. All of a sudden, I felt something touch my feet and my ankles. I saw nothing. I closed my eyes and it happened again. Only this time a voice said to me, "You are going to be all right." In no time, I could see better; the headache was gone; I wasn't stiff any more; I felt at peace. By the time the doctors came, I had no fever and my face was a happy face. I told them my story that Jesus had healed me. I am all right and I get great joy inside writing about this. It lets me know I can make it no matter what man says. Jesus has the last word. I give praise to Jesus and his father, God! Amen!

9

Other School Essays

I also wrote about how difficult it is to get a mortgage if you "had too much money."

"It seems so unfair because I feel that if you can pay five hundred and seventy five dollars a month for rent, you can pay the same for a mortgage payment. I feel that for honest working people the government should have some type of program to help people acquire ownership in a home. I'm not talking about some run-down dump in a bad neighborhood where people don't believe in helping themselves. I'm talking about something where you can look across the street and there's the Jones leaving for work or the Smiths having a nice family cookout."

Another essay was based on the big brick house with its wrought iron fence and big garage out back and the big cars and taxis which came there. It was Marguerite's of course, Charlottesville's well known brothel. My mama used to clean the downstairs rooms. She'd find gold watches and all kinds of jewelry laying on the chairs and tables. She put everything in a bag and gave it to the Madam. She said every furnishing was just beautiful. She knew the girls were too, but she didn't see them when she worked. Even though there was gold and fine furnishings, the Madam was less than generous to some people who worked for her. One man who cut the grass and was kind enough to put Marguerite's mail in a basket, which she lowered by rope from an upper story window, was asked to do some work on Christmas Day. He agreed although he wanted to be with his family. When it was time for him to leave, the Madam gave him a big envelope. Imagine his fury and disappointment when he opened it and found two quarters!

The house was finally auctioned, Marguerite having died in 1951. Then Miss "Blind" Jenny Jordan lived there for more than 20 years. I used to date her son Billy, so I knew about the house and the secret tunnel through which people made their getaways. When the house was demolished in November 1972, rumors of hidden monies proved true. So I wrote in my Albemarle High School essay this story: "The first blow from the machine sent money flying in the air and dropping to the ground like a hard rain. People stayed in that area for three months day and night—so much money found, it was incredible.

"At one corner of the black fence there was a square cement marker with capital B.C. on it. I know someone who dug and dug there and found thousands of dollars—enough to buy a house! This is true, and she's still living in it.

"Why would all these people say so many bad things about the road, yet they came to get our fortune. They called the road 'no good, poor trash' and everything you could think of. You know they're still there, but it is a different name now, Garrett Square.

"People came from all over Charlottesville and surrounding counties to find a fortune down there in Chinatown. Movie cameras, newspaper people, photographers, lawyers, doctors, you name it. They came in cars, trucks, buses, anything that would bring them. Picks, axes, shovels, hoes, sticks, anything that would help them to dig in the ground to find a fortune."

I know people found money. My former husband got $750 because he was one of the first on the scene.

Another place across the road from Marguerite's on Fifth Street was called the Stucco House. It was a big boarding house in which five families lived. There was only one toilet and everyone had to bring their own toilet paper. When you pushed the toilet seat down, water came up. In the yard was a spigot. There were buckets in the kitchen for water. There was no bathtub.

We kids could play ball, jacks, and marbles in the yard. But when the grownups came out, we had to leave. That's where the dice games took place. People would shoot craps until the police came and then run away. When this happened, we kids came back and picked up the money on the ground.

Some boys and men who lived in the Stucco House spent a lot of time trying to straighten their hair. They used a white cream substance that had lye in it. It had to be rinsed out at just the right time so you didn't get burned. Then your hair could be smoothed out or set back in careful waves using hair clips. A black scarf was tied around your head until it was set. This style was known as the conk. Now, conk started in the 1920's and lasted until the "natural look" in the 60's and 70's. The process was used in the movie "Malcolm X."

Now our house on Sixth Street SE did have running water but no bathtub. Every Sunday night a big tin tub was put in the living room next to the coal stove. Water was brought up from the basement, and I got the first bath because I was the youngest. Then came my sister Doris, then Mama and my father. We used Ivory Soap, but had no rinse water. When I was in grade school, my folks saved enough cash to have a bathroom installed. Daddy worked hard for his pay. Every two weeks he gave Mama all but five dollars. She ran the household.

When I want to go back in time, I sometimes stop in at the University of Virginia Hospital. There in a corridor near the emergency room entrance some paintings by Doris Collins are on display. One is a landscape of Virginia green fields; another is a peach orchard in delicate pink blooms; the red and white colors of the C & O station are forever bright in another. But best of all is the painting of houses on Sixth Street SE. Their stucco exteriors have an orange yellow tint and there on the front porch of the first house is a little figure in a red dress: Miss Maggie Rhodes, Tippy's mother. Next is the house of my grandfather, Bea Williams, and my uncle, Josh Grady. Standing on the porch of another house is Eddie Gates Possum. Last of all is a glimpse of Allen's store where we bought those thin pork chops. A strange thing happened one day when I brought my friend DR to see the painting of Sixth Street. It was a spur-of-the-moment visit, and as we stood there, amid a stream of people, one lady stopped and greeted us, remarking that she remembered Bea Williams and "that" was his house. Having grown up in Belmont, we had the surprising pleasure of shared recollections. All of us agreed that "progress" has destroyed more than neighborhoods and green spaces in Charlottesville. As we parted, she said, "You should write a book!" "We are," we answered, thinking how right it was that of all the people and of all the days in time, this was the one on which we met.

As we walked back to the parking garage, I was once again in our house, 519 Sixth Street SE. It was six o'clock in the morning and the door bell was ringing. "Please Mother Williams," said a child. "Do you have two slices of bread so my daddy can take lunch to work?" Mama would go to the kitchen and find the

```
              STATEMENT OF SALE BY
              Margaret W. Antrim
            to Hubert A. Williams and
              Dorothy Mae Williams
```

Sale closed as of September 27, 1956, date of deed.

Purchase price of property known
as 519 Sixth Street, S. E., in
Charlottesville, Virginia $ 2,500.00

Pro rata 1956 taxes (total tax
$16.53) total tax to be paid by Miss Antrim   4.13

Pro rata insurance   2.15

Cash payment $ 500.00

Bonds   2,000.00

Cash to balance paid by
purchaser   6.28
                                   _____
                                   $ 2,506.28 $ 2,506.28

Possession of premises has already been taken by the buyer.

Bought for $2500, the taxes were $16.53.

bread. Sometimes she'd give some money to the asker. Another morning, a young girl rang the bell, asking desperately, "Mother Williams, do you have an extra egg?" Another question came early one morning. "Mother Williams do you have some milk for my babies?" Mama gave some of her own money and sometimes money from the church's funds. "What is tithing for if the money can't be used for those in need?" she would say. This was her ministry when she lived on Sixth Street and later when she had a house on Grove Street. We had my brother's big green duffle bag containing his army stuff, and one day a man came in the snow and said, "I need some boots, badly." So Mama gave him the whole bag. He sat down and put on the boots right away. It helped him work and keep his family alive.

Talking to people, praying, giving was Mama's way of life both at her home, in jail, in nursing homes. She carried God's spirit to others. Mama used to tell us, "If you keep your hand closed, nothing will come in. If you keep it open and give, you'll receive in return, too." At Thanksgiving time, she'd cook enough for five families. All us kids packed boxes of food, having decorated them

with nice papers. At school time, she'd give book bags, socks, pencils. She "did" for the neighborhood.

While living on Grove Street, Mama had a "clothes give away" once a year, calling radio station WINA to invite people to 1004 Grove Street. She also had a "food give away." For this she invited firemen and policemen to come and pick up turkey dinners. We'd bake pound cake and sweet potato pies. We'd make macaroni and cheese dishes and potato salad. She'd put signs up on telephone poles and everybody came. "Bring your own bags" was the only requirement.

This house on Grove Street, the scene of Mama's preaching and source of all the good deeds of offering clothing and food, has had a terrible fate. On January 26, 2005, six young men broke into the house, smashing windows and doors, furniture, china and glass, tearing down the dining room chandelier, and breaking out the spindles on the staircase. Paint was spilled and it looked as though a fire was planned. I grieve for this vandalism, I feel as though my heart was broken along with the glass on the floor. Things will never be the same again.

10

Leaving School Behind

PHOTOGRAPHS taken at my Albemarle High School graduation keep everything very clear in my memory. One of the pictures shows my smiling Mama, who always wanted me to finish my education, and my husband, Norman Goins. Also there are my cute children: Archelle, Derek, and our twins Norman Jr. and Norkeita who were eight years old and students at Johnson School on Cherry Avenue. Archelle was eleven, enrolled at Buford, and Derek was just six, attending Johnson. I never missed a PTA meeting and was always at school, often helping the teachers in any way I could—like taking projects home. In 1985, I was voted mother of the year at Jackson-Via. I was awarded a basket of beautifully painted wooden apples. Mrs. Brightman and Mrs. Goodman nominated me for the award.

While I was so involved with my kids, I need to mention their Uncle Archie, my brother, who at this time was doing a remarkable thing for shut-ins, hospital patients and folks in jail. Archie spent 30 years of his life walking the streets of our town delivering mail. But he had another life, especially each Sunday morning starting at 8:00 a.m. He had met Kenneth White who operated gospel music stations in Washington, Culpepper and Warrenton and a gospel show in Charlottesville over radio station WELK. On Sundays in 1964, Archie learned to DJ shows for up to three hours—talking, playing records, and taking requests. "People, if it's important enough to talk about, it's important enough to write about. Drop me a line." He was swamped.

Archie announced community church news to listeners here, in Crozet, Nelson County and Buckingham County. Later he arranged gospel programs performed at churches and at Burley and Lane High auditoriums. Tickets were sold to defray costs of bringing singers here—like the Consolers, the Swanee Quintet and the Mighty Clouds of Joy. They were extraordinary. It was a great thing to have them appear in Charlottesville because the Clouds became famous, winning eleven Grammy awards, singing before Presidents Nixon and Carter, traveling all over the world. The Clouds have sung their gospel music in Carnegie Hall, Radio City Music Hall, Lincoln Center and the Kennedy Center. In 1999, they became only the second black quartet ever to be inducted into the Gospel Music Hall of Fame along with the Reverend Billy Graham.

And to think Archie "knew them when." I went to a party once where everyone treated me as a celebrity, just because I was Archie's sister and he meant so much to them.

On June 11, 2004, Archie passed at Martha Jefferson Hospital after a long illness. The Ebenezer Baptist Church on Sixth Street NW rang to the heavens with gospel music at his funeral.

Norman Eugene Goins

11

Finding Family

NOW, I could never finish talking about Norman. He is the best thing that ever happened to me—and a great husband and father. Born in Crozet to Mary Goins Barbour and Willie "Bird" Davis, Norman grew up in Charlottesville where he lived with the Catlett family on Lee Street in Gospel Hill. That's another all black section located behind the University of Virginia Hospital.

He lost track of his mother until a very strange thing happened to both of us. One day I was shopping in Kroger's, Barracks Road, and I noticed a woman in a white uniform who was also collecting groceries. I couldn't stop looking at her because in her face I saw my husband's features. So finally I begged her pardon and asked if she had a son, Norman. Quite startled, she said, "Yes, but I haven't seen him in a long time."

"I know where he is," I said as we stared at each other. "He is right over there working at the Gaslight

Restaurant. Will you go to see him?"

"He doesn't hate me? Will he talk to me?" she asked.

"Norman talks about you all the time," I answered. "He has never stopped talking about you, and wonders about you. Will you go to see him?"

"Not today," she replied, "but who are you that you know me?"

So I told her, I was Norman's wife. She was working as a live-in housekeeper in Farmington and promised to go to meet her son the next Thursday when she came to town. I went on my way, but didn't tell Norman of this strange meeting. I just couldn't.

Then it all came true, because she did go to the Gaslight. And when Norman saw her they were suddenly hugging and crying in front of all the customers. She lived in Waynesboro and later we and our children visited her for several years! Our son Derek was born on the day that she died.

Norman later found his brothers and sisters who lived in Crozet, Brown's Cove and Maryland. He was no longer a lone boy who finished high school and spent six years in the U.S. Navy, serving mostly in the Mediterranean area.

Now though Norman and I knew each other, we met finally at work in a cleaner's store. We went to a party at 518 South Street. I remember it so well: Norman looking handsome in his white shirt and green plaid trousers. I was wearing a pretty black dress. We danced and danced to the tune "When Something Is Wrong With My Baby, Something Is Wrong With Me." We dated steadily after that—it must have been 1969 or

1970.

But back to news of Derek, our little son, now a handsome young man, who is a student at Norfolk State University after graduating from Charlottesville High School in 2002. He is now studying business and entrepreneurship, hoping to operate a clothing and sporting goods store here. He will become the first member of our family to earn a college degree. I was just bursting with pride on May 12, 2004 when I attended a Chamber of Commerce luncheon at Doubletree. Derek was one of four recipients of $2000 stipends made possible by the Charlottesville scholarship program established by Charlottesville City Council through appropriations and supplemented with funds raised by a volunteer board. It is managed by the Charlottesville-Albemarle Community Foundation. The room was filled with elected officials and business leaders. Everyone welcomed the students and their family representatives with great kindness. A picture of the students was published in the Tribune's May 20th issue. Now in 2005 on May 17 Norman had the opportunity to enjoy this ceremony because Derek received a $2000 scholarship for 2005. He was one of just two students so honored in a repeat funding.

Dorothy May Williams and Hubert Allen Williams

12

Children and More Children

MY family has had its joys and sorrows, and being a big family we've had more than our share. But God has given us the strength to see them through. "Stand straight and know that God is with you," Mama told me. Just when Mama and Dad were set to retire at age 60, they opened their home and hearts to four little children, three girls and a boy. They were the children of my sister Diane. She was "the wild one" of the family and was unable and unwilling to care for them. She wanted "to be free." Later on she had three more little girls with a different father. And again the girls were going to have to go to foster homes. So Norman and I took them in. We bought bunk beds so each child would have its own place to lay its head. We raised seven children. This story is very sad because, through their mother's influence, the three girls we legally adopted are no longer living with us, even though we must support them financially. This will take some prayer and patience and more prayer and probably a lawyer. The story seems to have no end. But we were continuing to care for our family's children in our own houses. Years before this, Doris and her husband were working hard to earn a living, and sent their twin sons to the country to be under Grandpa's eye and under Grandma's loving care and good cooking.

Well, I used to give my folks a little time to themselves on the weekends when I took "the first four" over to my house. It was a circus—and lots of chicken to fry. I was working full time at home as well as at Martha Jefferson Hospital, first in the cafeteria and then in the operating room. One night Norman and I had a big, really big argument. I went to work without speaking and slammed the door behind me. That morning in the middle of work, I was called down to the emergency room. Norman had had a heart attack! He came out okay because he knew he had to help me with those seven children. I came out okay too, thanking God and knowing you should never, never go to bed angry enough to smother all your words, and never leave your home without apologizing.

13

When We Were Young

BEING so busy with jobs and just life in general, there was just no time for all the fun I'd had in my twenties. I remember dancing every Friday and Saturday nights! There were two places to go: the Odd Fellows Hall on Market Street where you couldn't buy liquor and the Elks around the corner where beer was sold. Those were the days when there was "a drink in the car" brought by the boys, who wanted it, or a drink from a bottle in the girls' purses. Even uptown folks had to bring their bottles in brown paper bags if they wanted drinks at their parties. That was Virginia law. The bands belted out rock and roll all evening and I earned my name "Snake Hips" by dancing under the limbo sticks as they got lower and lower to the floor. I know I saw Norman there, but I never danced with him.

The Odd Fellows Hall was a brick building a couple of stories high which later became the site of the Pentecostal True Holiness Church. The pastor was Bishop

Robert J. Michie, and my Mama attended services there. There was a big room on the second floor where meals were shared. The church eventually moved to Altavista Avenue.

Speaking of churches—I mentioned the one on Vinegar Hill we passed going home from Jefferson School. Well, the Reverend Frank Jackson came down on Sundays from Washington D.C. where he drove a taxi cab for a living. The church doors were always open in the summer so anyone could come in to worship or just sit. They had a great fund-raiser idea there. There were buckets of lemons and you could say you would offer a dime, a quarter, but mostly it was a dime, for each seed found in the lemon when it was cut. So you paid 50 or 70 or just 20 cents! Lots of lemonade was made as well as funds were raised!

But back to Bishop Michie who inspired several young men, including my brother Archie, to find ways to improve the Sixth Street neighborhood. Tallying the number of families and children with Archie were Theodore Johnson, Marshal Allen, Jessie Williams and Rosa Mae Barber. Results of the canvas helped to establish a daycare center at Hope House, 438 Sixth Street SE, where Bishop Michie held church services. It expanded later to the C.H. Williams warehouse. Laura Wilson became the center's teacher, assisted by Rosa. Theodore taught "Fun with Music," an afternoon program. Of course it's no longer there. Only memories of Sixth Street remain along with the area once called "Happy Hollow" which included Parrott Street and Diggs Street. This is where we used to comb the bushes and stream to collect tin cans and scrap iron. We took it to Coiner's Scrap Yard in exchange for a dollar. Conway Alley, off Ware Street, is not there either. Gone too is Mrs. Marshall's. This was a store we kids loved to go to with my Daddy. On Thursday afternoons, often as not, Daddy gathered up the "chillens" on Sixth Street and went on to the store built of rocks, next to the rock house in which Mrs. Marshall lived. He'd had his pay from IX and Company, so we were allowed each to have a little bag for the candy or ginger snaps which we chose. We had a real treat in the popsicles she sold. Daddy liked vanilla coated in chocolate and we liked vanilla with real strawberries or vanilla with real bananas inside. Daddy would start out with just my sister and me, but by the time we would get to the store, sometimes there would be ten or fifteen "chillens." The store was always open and if you needed a loaf of bread or some moon pies, you knew where to go.

Dorothy May Williams and Hubert Allen Williams

14

New Crossroads

NOW we come to a big crossroad in my "Pathways of Life" story. I became housekeeper for Mr. and Mrs. Bruce Sherman who lived in a brick mansion on Rugby Road. When their grandchildren Hugh, Jimmy and little Dave visited, I took care of them. They were the children of their daughter Mary Motley Kalergis and her husband David. The caring continued first at Fox Ridge Farm in Albemarle County when the family completed their move from New York. Later they built a house at Sugarday Farm and I had their little daughter Natasha to tend and love. Norman was also employed to help maintain the houses and properties.

One day Mr. Sherman came into the kitchen where I was working and asked me if I realized I was famous! "Me? How could this be?" "Look," he said showing me the May 1987 issue of "The Ladies Home Journal." In it was a picture of me and my little children taken by Mary Kalergis and part of an article on page 43: "Mothers Talk About Mothering . . . " "Our gift to you: a special photo essay in honor of Mother's Day by Mary Motley Kalergis." Under this picture was this caption: "Having a child can certainly change you for better or worse. I used to be pretty wild and on the go, but since I had my kids, I just wanted to stay home. I think I was always longing for something, and when I had a baby, I felt that I'd found it. I feel calmness and better about myself. Nothing can separate us."

This picture also appeared in the book "Mother: A Collective Portrait" by Mary Motley Kalergis, published by E.P. Dutton, New York: 1987. The story on page 67 opposite the photograph recounts the death in sleep of my sister's baby boy and my Mama's help in caring for my children when I needed her. I said, "A woman's most important job is to hold the family together. I plan on watching my own grandchildren. We are a family that pulls together. Nothing can separate us."

Now Mary, who became a famous photographer, told me she was working on a book—a book about people of all persuasions and who represented many aspects of life. When she met my mother, it was an instant of mutual regard. We all treasure their friendship and the beautiful photographs of Dorothy and Buster Williams in Mary's two books. One is "Charlottesville Portrait" published by Howell Press of Charlottesville in 2000. On page 88, there is a picture of Mama and Daddy. A caption and picture on page 89 states: "Dorothy Williams at the pulpit in her front parlour, Fifeville, 1990." Another book is "With This Ring: A Portrait of Marriage" by Mary Motley Kalergis, the Chrysler Museum of Art, Norfolk, Virginia: 1997. On page 121, the caption for the picture of Mama and Daddy says: "I must tell you that life is hard." The preceding page says, "Married more than 60 years. She runs the Born Again Holiness Pentecostal Church on Sundays. They also care for their grandchildren, six of whom are living with them at the time of this portrait."

"Dorothy: the reason so many women are alone today is because they left God out of the plan. He teaches us to do the right thing. Then some men leave no matter what you do. Buster: You can drive a man away if you ask too much of him. A man cannot carry a woman on his back." Also on page 80 of "With This Ring," there is a photograph of Norman and Deloris Goins. Imagine! The caption reads: "For some reason, it seems like some people can't learn things without suffering." I am quoted as saying: "It took a heart attack for us to stop taking each other for granted." Norman also tells everyone, "It makes you a better person." Our copy of "With This Ring" has Mary Kalergis's autograph with the inscription: "Norman and Deloris Goins. They are sometime employees and long-time friends."

I know the Kalergis family rejoiced with my family later in 2003 when Norman received a great honor. He had been employed at Martha Jefferson Hospital for more than eight years in the food service department. And lo and behold! He was recognized as the best support employee of the year. Mr. James Haden, MJH President, presented him with a plaque and a check for $500 at the awards banquet held at the Omni Hotel. I was and am so proud of him, just as he is of the letter he received from Mitch Van Yahres on Commonwealth of Virginia House of Delegates letterhead paper congratulating him on receiving the president's award. "You are part of what makes Martha Jefferson such an excellent hospital and what makes our community such a wonderful place to live."

Can you imagine how wonderful it is to bring to life your mama and daddy by seeing their photographs at the University of Virginia Art Museum or hanging up in a permanent collection of Mary Kalergis's works at the Virginia National Bank on Emmet Street? They are also in a museum in Texas.

Upstairs in the bank building is a picture of a man sitting in a rocking chair. He's Dallas Garland, another study from "Charlottesville Portrait." The caption reads: "Father of nine children, 54 grandchildren, 78 great-grandchildren, 46 great-great-grandchildren, and 12 great-great-great-grandchildren, 1994." My cousin Adelay married Robert, one of his sons!

Another book we cherish in our home on Cherry Avenue is "The Circle of Enduring Love" by Pat Ross, Andrews McNeal Publishing, Kansas City: 1998. Opposite the picture on page 42 is this caption: "Buster and Dorothy Williams now married more than sixty years when this photograph was taken." Photograph copyright Mary Motley Kalergis, Charlottesville, Virginia. On page 13 of this book are words written by Maria Edgeworth, 1814: "The human heart at whatever age opens only to the heart that opens in return."

I've opened my heart many, many times. I've been lucky to have loved and cared for many children other than my own family. In the 1970's two little boys were special: Jeffrey and Derek Morris. I named my own son Derek after him.

Mary Kalergis took this picture of my family (Derek, Norman, Norkeita, Archelle, Norman Jr., and Deloris) one Sunday afternoon in our front yard.

Through Mary Kalergis's contacts I came to care for Ches Goodall on Rosser Lane—the beginning of several little ones in the Rugby Road area. It's been about ten years. Some of my children have been Ches Goodall, Annabel Jones, George and Martha Sawyer, Jackson and Thomas Jones, Molly, Willis and Nonie Bocock, Stafford and Andrew Vaughn, Huyler and Reeves Dunn, and Alex and Marlon Johnson. Now I drive the car for an elderly lady on Rosser Lane as well as helping her in other ways. She claims this is a "second childhood" episode!

15

Dreams

NOW you never know how long it takes to realize not all but even some of your dreams. All my life I have wanted to ride in a big-powered, low-slung Corvette and now I have. On Thursday September 2, 2004 at 6:50 p.m., I stepped into one, a convertible Corvette with a stick-shift in the floor and a driver named Josh, grandson of my elderly lady on Rosser Lane. I felt like a celebrity riding with the top down in this cool, cool car. People were just looking at me in surprise. I knew what they were thinking: what is this black, grey-haired lady doing cruisin' with this young, good-looking white boy? I really got the biggest kick when we drove up to my house on Cherry Avenue and my neighbor came running out to see me. I introduced Josh as my new boyfriend who came down from New York to visit me. I'll never forget the look on her face. Just shock. When I told her who Josh really was, she laughed so hard, just loving it. What a nice day in my life. I shall never forget it. Maybe Josh will come again and we'll go like the wind down some highway with my hair blowing back from my face as I see the dream coming true.

Dreams of another kind have come true in Charlottesville. I am proud to have voted for the first black mayor in the city, Charles Barbour in May 1974, and also for Virginia's first black governor, Douglas Wilder. I walk now across a bridge on West Main Street named for Drewery Brown, Charlottesville's activist who worked to establish Hope House and the Community Action Program. Our family has always exercised our rights as citizens. My mama and daddy rose early on election days to cast their ballots. I do so today. Life and relationships are never perfect, but it is, indeed, a better world we have today when black and white persons can enjoy friendships and break bread together.

16

Recipes, Past and Present

WHEN Grandpa said, "A-a-amen. Let's eat!" Grandma often brought to the table:

Spoon Bread

She'd mixed some handfuls of corn meal with a cup of spring water brought to the boil. She added milk, two eggs and some lard, putting it all into a greased bowl. This went into the wood stove oven to bake about half an hour.

Now-a-days Deloris measures:

$\frac{3}{4}$ cup House Autry corn meal mix
3 tablespoons Crisco

1 cup boiling tap water
1 cup milk
2 eggs, well beaten

She mixes the meal and shortening, slowly adding boiling water, beating until smooth. Then she adds milk and eggs, mixing well, pours it into a greased bowl and bakes for 30 to 40 minutes in a 350-375 degree oven.

Fried Green Tomatoes

Grandma picked seven or eight tomatoes in the garden before they ripened, sliced them up and dredged them in a flour and cornmeal mixture to which she had added chopped onion and garlic, salt and pepper. She fried them in hot lard until they turned golden brown in the iron skillet.

Deloris mixes:

$\frac{1}{2}$ cup corn meal
$\frac{1}{2}$ cup flour
$\frac{1}{2}$ cup cooking oil
1 teaspoon onion powder
1 teaspoon garlic powder
1 teaspoon salt
1 teaspoon pepper

She slices seven or eight green tomatoes, dredges them

and fries until golden brown using $\frac{1}{2}$ cup of cooking oil.

Fried Fresh Corn

This is the way Grandma fixed my favorite breakfast after I went to the garden and picked some ears of corn. She cut down the corn kernels and fried them in fatback or lard in a hot skillet, adding water and cornstarch. Sometimes there was some country ham, sometimes not.

Deloris cooks it like this:

> Corn on the cob
> Country ham
> 1 teaspoon cornstarch
> Salt and pepper to taste
> Butter or vegetable oil
> $\frac{1}{2}$ cup water

She removes corn from cob while cooking a couple of country ham slices in frying pan with a little butter or oil. When ham is done, she adds the corn, salt and pepper, covers and cooks about fifteen minutes stirring a little. She adds water and corn starch and cooks to her desired consistency.

Fish-for-Dinner

Grandma got out the skillet, lard and corn meal when there was fish for dinner. Grandpa caught the fish from the Rivanna River bank. He had a hook and string on a pole, a stake stuck into the ground near the river edge and several shorter strings, each attached to a sharp, pointed little stick. When he landed a fish he used the pointed stick to pierce the fish's mouth and come out of the gills. The strings were tied to the stake and the fish-for-dinner were put into the river to keep cool until it was time to walk or hitch a ride home. He fished all year long. Grandma washed the catch, and then put it in buttermilk for an hour. She coated them with a cornmeal mix containing onion, garlic, salt and pepper and some bay seasoning. They sizzled in the pan until golden brown. Grandma ate all of the fish serving, including bones, head and the eyes! Sometimes shad was purchased and fried in lard also.

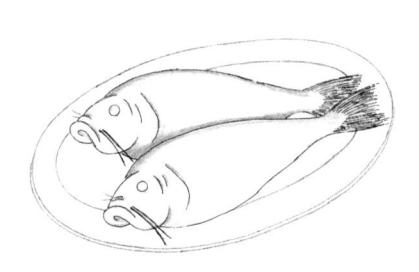

Now Deloris has this recipe for her family:

Fried Catfish, eight servings. She uses:

    2 cups of milk
    2 cups yellow corn meal
    3-4 teaspoons pepper
    2 teaspoons onion powder

2 teaspoons garlic powder
2 teaspoons old bay seasoning
Dash salt
Vegetable oil

She washes and dries the catfish, then soaks them in milk for one half hour. She removes the fish, shaking off the milk, and coats them in the cornmeal mixture. They are fried in a skillet or deep fryer until golden brown, then drained on a rack. "It's good!"

Hoe Cakes

One of our favorite suppers was fried apples and farm-made sausages with hoe cakes. Grandma didn't measure ingredients. She just knew how big a scoop of lard was needed, and how many handfuls of flour. She blended them with a fork and added just the right amount of buttermilk. With her hands she shaped balls of dough—pretty large ones, because after all these were "hoe" cakes—put them on a baking sheet and baked them brown. We ate these wonders with cups of buttermilk. This is indeed a memory, for my kids never had such yummy enjoyment.

Another treat of Grandma's was applesauce pie. She made the crust with lard and flour, then piled in cored, peeled apples which were softening (but not spoiled), topped it with sugar, spices and butter. That wood stove oven did produce the very best of flavors!

Wild Game

When Grandpa wasn't farmin', fishin' or choppin' wood, he took his gun and went off into the woods. Several hours later he had found dinner for everyone: rabbit, squirrel, ground hog, or quail. His gunny sack was always pretty full. The animals were hung, hind feet first, on the clothes line. Grandpa sharpened his big knife, and started to cut around the feet, then pulled the hide down, gutted the critters and it was off with the heads! Grandma then cut the meat into portions to be soaked in salt water. In a batter of flour, salt and pepper, they were fried until brown. Water and onions (green ones in season) covered them and they baked in the oven. Rice or boiled potatoes and string beans made the meal.

The birds were quail and were popped into a tub of boiling water for a few minutes so the feathers could be plucked readily. There was a big table outdoors, covered with newspaper, where they were gutted and beheaded. They were boiled until tender with garlic and onions. Again, Grandma used flour for thickening and served the quail with some kind of cooked greens like turnip or beet tops.

The groundhog was skinned, gutted, washed and placed in a baking pan, and then he was roasted in the oven several hours as you would do a ham. I never really liked the brownish meat very much, but it was eaten right down to the bones.

Scrambled Eggs and Pork Brains

We didn't really want to join Grandma when she cooked this favorite of hers.

> Pork brains
> 1 onion
> Salt and pepper to taste
> Lard or butter
> Eggs

Sautee onion in lard or butter. Add pork brain and cook for about five minutes. Beat eggs and add to onion and brains. Cook until eggs are done. Salt and pepper to taste. Dig in!

Fried Potatoes with Scrambled Eggs

> Potatoes
> 1 onion, diced
> Eggs
> Salt to taste
> Pepper to taste
> Lard

Peel and slice potatoes. Wash and drain them. Add lard to skillet and get skillet medium hot. Add potatoes and diced onion. Let cook and cover for about ten minutes. Add salt and pepper to taste. Stir and recover for about another ten to fifteen minutes. Take cover off and cook until potatoes have a touch of brown. Add beaten eggs and cook until eggs are done. (We liked this one!)

Chicken Feet Stew

Grandma needed chicken feet, salt and pepper, onions, garlic flour and water. She washed the chicken feet very well before putting them in a big pot of water with onion, salt, pepper and garlic. This cooked for about forty-five minutes. Flour was added to the pot for thickening and everything cooked uncovered for about ten minutes. You can cook the same way today if you can buy chicken feet at the grocery store.

Corn Bread

    1 cup self-rising corn meal
    2 eggs
    1 8 oz. can cream style corn
    1 cup sour cream
    $\frac{1}{2}$ cup salad oil
    Sugar to taste

Combine all ingredients, mixing well. Pour into a greased nine inch pan and bake at 400 for 20-30 minutes. Bring out the butter!!

Pie Crust

    2 cups flour
    1 tsp salt
    $\frac{2}{3}$ cup shortening

With some cold water in bowl, mix flour, shortening and salt with a fork until crumbs are course. Add about four to six tablespoons water, a little at a time until you can make a nice ball with dough. Roll half the ball with rolling pin on a lightly dusted surface. Lay on pie pan, add fruit, add top crust and trim edges and crimp edges. Prick top crust. Bake at about 400 for thirty to forty minutes.

Sweet Potato Pie

    2-lbs can of sweet potatoes
    1 stick butter, softened
    3 eggs
    $1\frac{1}{2}$ cups sugar
    2 tsp vanilla
    1 tsp nutmeg
    $\frac{1}{4}$ tsp cinnamon
    1 tsp lemon extract

$1\frac{1}{2}$ cups "half and half" or evaporated milk
Dash of salt

If you use canned potatoes, drain juice from potatoes. (Or you can use fresh sweet potatoes. Maybe two pounds. If using fresh potatoes, boil in jackets until soft. Let cool, then remove skins.) Then mash lumps with beater. Add eggs and beat for about two minutes. Add sugar, softened butter, salt, nutmeg, vanilla, cinnamon, lemon extract. Then beat about two minutes. Add milk and blend very well. Pour into an unbaked pie shell (do not put a top crust on this pie). Bake at 350 for about fifty minutes or until brown.

Pound Cake

$\frac{1}{2}$ cup plain Crisco
2 sticks butter
3 cups sugar
5 large eggs
3 cups all-purpose flour
1 cup sweet milk
2 tsp vanilla
2 tsp lemon

Oven 350. Soften Crisco and butter. Gradually add sugar. Add eggs one at a time. Alternate flour and milk. It's better to put the lemon and vanilla in the milk. Bake in a greased tube cake pan until golden brown.

Doris's Cream Puffs

    1 stick margarine
    1 cup all purpose flour
    1 cup water
    4 eggs
    $\frac{1}{4}$ teaspoon salt
    2 boxes vanilla pudding
    3 cups milk
    Confectioner's sugar

Bake at 350 degrees. In a saucepan, add 1 cup water, 1 stick margarine. Boil. Remove from heat. Add flour and stir well. Cool for a few minutes and then add eggs one at a time. Stir very well after each one. Spoon and swirl on lightly greased cookie sheet. This should make about 12 shells. A tablespoon is great to use. Bake at 350 degrees until golden brown. Remove from oven and stick shells with a small knife to vent air. Cool. *Cream filling* Use 2 boxes of vanilla pudding and three cups milk. Beat well. Let set for about 5 minutes. Cut shells and fill with pudding. Sprinkle with confectioner's sugar.

Afterward

The White Cat of Rosser Lane

When we began these stories I wrote in the foreword that Deloris promised to tell why she's afraid of cats.

So here goes.

> Roller skating was a passion with me when I was ten years old. I wore right through the wheels on several pairs.

One evening I skated into a hallway at Hope House, 438 Sixth Street SE. It was dark and as I headed toward a back door I struck something. A big something with sharp claws and teeth. A big black tom cat who, I know now, was as scared as I was. He attacked my face and arms and I think my screams. Neighbors came running and my daddy rescued me.

I've never patted a cat or talked to one until now.

The beautiful, white cat who lives with my elderly lady greets me at the door to "her" house and expects me to touch her head and back.

And much to my family's disbelief, I do.

My bravery is bolstered by the knowledge that she believes that I am her friend. I must say, though, that I'm glad she's soft and white—not big and black. Besides, she doesn't have any claws in the front paws.